Teacher's Selection:
Anthology of Fifth Grade Poetry

2000 Edition
Volume VI

Published by Anthology of Poetry, Inc.

Teacher's Selection:
Anthology of Fifth Grade Poetry©
2000 Edition
Volume VI

Printed in the United States of America

Authors responsible for originality
of poems submitted.

The Anthology of Poetry, Inc.
P.O. Box 698 • 307 East Salisbury
Asheboro, NC   27204-0698

ISBN: 1-883931-22-3

The 2000 edition of the *Teacher's Selection: Anthology of Fifth Grade Poetry* proved to be as exciting and as diverse as our past editions. All subjects are represented. The poets have given us a look at their world. It's full of monsters, best friends, strange adults, snowflakes, dinosaurs, the big game, the first rumblings of romance and concern about the world they will inherit. Only poetry could contain the explosive energy of a child's mind. The poetry of this edition demonstrates again that poetry is the best medium for young writers to express themselves.

The Anthology of Poetry proudly presents to you the hard bound edition of *Teacher's Selection: Anthology of Fifth Grade Poetry*. The poems of this edition are the top honors from fifth grade classrooms from across the United States. Of all entries from each school only a few receive nominations for publication by each fifth grade teacher. And of those nominations only three are selected for publication. Congratulations.

We thank the fifth grade teachers for their participation in this project and, as always, we applaud the poets who shared their gifts.

We look forward to the publication of upcoming editions of *Teacher's Selection: Anthology of Fifth Grade Poetry*.

The Editors

April Showers

When the sun is strong and the day is hot,
Kids come out and play a lot.
Well in the spring, it is the same way.
It is a merry season with bunny-shaped clouds
all through the day.
This is the season with bugs and flowers.
It is also the season where birds take rain showers.
It is the happiest season all through the year.
It is the season when soft wind tickles your ear.

Tiffany McIntosh

New Preparatory Middle School
Jamaica, NY
Nominated by fifth grade teacher Ms. Kessler

What I Miss

I miss the days of laughs and plays
Even though now I have different ways
My mom is barely there for touch and see
All there is me... me... me

There is no time for love and care
Because she is barely even there
If only fate for me had a different course
Then my feelings might come from a different source

I wish good times could repeat itself
But I guess it's only a memory stacked high on a shelf
I guess these things weren't meant to be
But I wonder if fate will change for me

Jonathan Talmi

Public School 117 Q
Briarwood, NY
Nominated by fifth grade teacher Susan Berkson

The Secret Lives Of Snowmen

The snowmen are fresh,
Just made today,
Jumping around, wanting to play.

Throwing snowballs at everyone,
Trying to have a little fun.
Running around, all over town,
Acting like several goofy clowns.

The snowmen and snow ladies
Are dancing together,
In such wonderful, beautiful weather.

Children are watching, wanting to play,
Wishing this would happen every day.

Kate Bratskeir

Buckley Country Day School
Roslyn, NY
Nominated by fifth grade teachers
Matthew Leaf and Peter Carioscia

A New Morning

Early morning's rising.
The sun is but a glow,
New shadows dance happily
Upon the wintry snow.

I can't ever understand,
And know I never will,
About this great feeling,
Momentous and still.

I'm living in a painting
That exists within my mind,
Living in a moment
Of its own place and time.

Annick Marie Thomas

Buckley Country Day School
Roslyn, NY
Nominated by fifth grade teachers
Matthew Leaf and Peter Carioscia

Initial Poem

R ushing raindrops,
D azzling rainbows mix with
M ajestic dawns.

R acing dancers,
D ancing angels dance on
M ystical sunrays.

R iver leaves,
D aytime sunsets bring
M arching clouds.

Ritchlyn Darielle Mohammed

All Saints Regional Catholic School
Glen Cove, NY
Nominated by fifth grade teacher Judith Tonner

Snow

Snow
white soft
drifting melting falling
cold fun
Snow

Alexandra Arthus

All Saints Regional Catholic School
Glen Cove, NY
Nominated by fifth grade teacher Judith Tonner

Birds

Have you ever wondered why birds can fly?
Or why they have such wonderful eyes?
Well, there's a secret that nobody knows,
Which started very long ago.

Man was created with intelligent minds,
Made by God to be His very own kind.
He loved us better than any others,
And protected us by making guardian mothers.

So whenever you see a bird flying by,
It's probably your guardian angel in disguise.
And don't throw rocks,
Or scare them away,
Because these undercover angels are here to stay.

Amanda Raposo

Buckley Country Day School
Roslyn, NY
Nominated by fifth grade teachers
Matthew Leaf and Peter Carioscia

I Know...

I know that I'm still young,
And that I have lots more to grow.
I know that to drugs,
I should always say no.

I know that the sun,
Shines brightly down on me.
I know that all these things,
You and I can both see.

I know that the river,
Flows to the edge of the earth.
I know before a baby,
There is always a birth.

I know that in my heart,
There is room for each one.
I know you should never,
Look straight at the sun.

I know that my dreams,
Will always come true.
If they wouldn't I'd be lost,
What about you?

Lisa Shapiro

Hebrew Academy of the Five Towns
Lawrence, NY
Nominated by fifth grade teacher Rachelle Neuman

Who I Am

I am beautiful and beautiful is my name.
I am a child and my eyes are dark brown.
Sometimes life is hard
But I try not to frown.
I am beautiful and beautiful is my name.

Latonya Kelley

M. G. Rhodes Elementary School
Hempstead, NY
Nominated by fifth grade teacher Claude Ervin

Quiet Time

I like when I can take a break,
And go outside and just relax.
Sometimes I read a book,
And also help my mother cook.
Sometimes I dream of foreign places,
And running fast, and winning races.

Quiet time is treasured time,
Pleasant, peaceful, positive time.
Time without shouts and stresses.
Time away from fuss and messes.

Quiet time is my time.

Stephanie Lauren Meissner

Hebrew Academy of the Five Towns
Lawrence, NY
Nominated by fifth grade teacher Muriel Barber

Emotion

Anger seems RED
Like rivers of gasoline seeping into a flaming forest
I see a horrible thermal nuclear explosion
I hear the yells of the helpless victims
I smell black disgusting smog
I touch my fist against my hand
I taste revenge and hatred.

Charles Agricola

West End School
Lynbrook, NY
Nominated by fifth grade teacher Mary Ann Midiri

Watching Sports

Lots and lots and lots of sports
My brother plays sports
Always sitting in the stands
Blocking balls with my hands
So confusing back and forth
I don't know what it's worth
Watching cluelessly in a daze
Never aware when the ball comes ablaze
Congratulating teams all the time
I wish this poem were easier to rhyme

Lauren Bencivenga

West End School
Lynbrook, NY
Nominated by fifth grade teacher Jenny Lee

As the bright, glistening fish swim to the
watery deep,

As the eternal flowers grow in the mass
grasslands,

As the birds sing their enchanting songs
of season,

As the tasteful fruits of the blossoming trees
emerge,

As the church bells unite and form their soothing
chimes,

As the damp, misty rain falls onto lifeful
earth,

You will notice,
life is of only
laughter
and cheer.

Mathew Harrison

Cross Street School
Williston Park, NY
Nominated by fifth grade teacher Karen Carraro

13

Doodles

a squiggle a dot,
a line and a spot,
a shape of a square,
a long line of hair,
some flowers and roses,
people with great long noses,
if you're sitting around draw a town,
use a squiggle a dot,
a line and a spot!!

Cassandra Olivos

Cross Street School
Williston Park, NY
Nominated by fifth grade teacher Karen Carraro

I Like To Eat Ice Cream

I like to eat ice cream,
Pizza I digest;
Bagels are very good,
And cheese is always best.

I will eat spinach,
I like all kinds of meat;
I'm not a picky eater,
But broccoli I won't eat.

Bribe me, force me,
It won't do any good;
To you it may taste heavenly,
To me it tastes like wood.

I'll never, never eat it,
Even it'll improve my weight;
You'll give me ice cream if I eat some?
Please pass me the plate.

Tamar Chatzinoff

Torah Academy for Girls
Far Rockaway, NY
Nominated by fifth grade teacher Debbie Waltuch

Oh, If You Would Listen...

There may once come a time
when you'll appreciate the sound,
of a little ant crawling on the ground.

Or it may be the sound of buzzing bees,
or the sound of swaying trees.

It may be the sound of splashing seas,
or the sound of annoying fleas.

It may be the sound of crackling leaves
under your feet,
or maybe children munching a treat.

There are so many sounds to appreciate,
you just have to go investigate.

You will hear alarm clocks ringing,
or radios singing.

You will hear storms coming,
or thunder rumbling.

You will hear people talking,
or going walking.

Oh, there are such wonderful noises,
just listen closely and hear their voices.

Of engines roaring,
and of people snoring.

Of volcanoes erupting,
and of earthquakes grumbling.

Of birds chirping,
and of frogs burping.

Oh, I can just go on forever,
but now I'll move on to my next endeavor.

Chevie Liss

Torah Academy for Girls
Far Rockaway, NY
Nominated by fifth grade teacher Beth Lieberstein

The Adirondacks

The day awaits us
An adventurous, fun day
In the Adirondacks.

The car ride:
Four long, hot, sticky, sweaty hours in the car.
But worth it.

The scenery, beautiful:
Gorgeous mountains raise their heads to the sky.
The trees swaying with the wind.

We drive up to the cabin.
The cabin filled with happy memories.
We unpack our bags.
My dad promises that we will go fishing
In our secret spot.

My brothers go hiking.
Mom, Sarah and I go antiquing.
The stores are filled with antiques.
Beautiful treasures piled into one store.
I love this time together.
Just Mom, Sarah and me.

My brothers and Dad tackle the treacherous mountain.
They climb the steep land.
Sweat pouring down their backs.
Heavy loads on their backs.
But when they reach the top,
They feel like three kings!

When the day's adventure is almost over,
We start up the fishing boat.
My heart pounding with excitement.
Longing to get my hands on that rod.
We sail out on Paradox Lake.
We land in our secret spot.
I drop my line in.
Plop.
I sit and wait.
Waiting for that nibble.
I feel a nibble.
A BITE!
I try to reel it in.
The fish is so BIG and HEAVY!
Finally (with Dad's help) I reel it in.
"I just caught a 12-inch long trout!"
My hook gone.
My rod bent.
The boat has water in it,
But I am still happy that I caught that amazing trout.

We sail back
And let the fish go.
A campfire is started.
We toast marshmallows.
Then Dad tells the story of Tim Tyler!
The man who killed his family and goes crazy
Whenever he sees the color RED!
We are scared even though we know it's not true.

We return to the cabin.
Longing for a good night's rest.
Another day awaits us.
Another fun, adventurous day in the Adirondacks.

Rachel Vorsanger

Public School 1140
Belle Harbor, NY
Nominated by fifth grade teacher Fran Langbaum

When The Water Is Silent

When the water is silent,
So am I.
There are no waves.
There is no movement.
When the water is silent,
It looks like delicate glass,
So peaceful and quiet.
When the water is silent,
You can close your eyes,
And feel the warm, gentle sun
On your face.
When the water is silent,
So is the world to me.
There is no limit to my imagination,
When the water is silent.

Meghan Ashley Brolly

Public School 1140
Belle Harbor, NY
Nominated by fifth grade teacher Ann Marie Todes

Lazy Flowers

Spring flowers are poking up from the ground
Tulips and daffodils all around
Pussy willows now meowing their praise
Dogwoods barking a lot these days
Crocus croaking forsythia and violet today
They're enjoying it in everyway
Summer flowers won't be here for daisies
"Wow," said the spring flowers, "They sure are lazy!"

Danielle Palumbo

Woods Road School
North Babylon, NY
Nominated by fifth grade teacher Marilyn Corso

Spring Sounds

Birds chirping
Bees buzzing
Lawn mowers zooming
Cars honking

Ice-cream truck bells ringing
Children yelling
Wind howling
Rain pittering-pattering

Frogs croaking
Cats meowing
Dogs barking
Friends shouting

Spring is here!

Kelly Mahoney

Woods Road School
North Babylon, NY
Nominated by fifth grade teacher Marilyn Corso

The Toy

Once there was this boy,
He liked one special toy,
He played with it day and night,
Wouldn't let it out of his sight,
It filled his heart with joy.

Zachary L. Carroll

Woods Road School
North Babylon, NY
Nominated by fifth grade teacher Jennifer Ferer

The Snowman

Hooray for the cold weather
Hooray for the snow!
I'm going to build a snowman
So outside I go!
It takes a lot of work to build him
At least a few hours go by
I need a ladder to put the last snowball on
He must be seven feet high.
Mom calls me in for dinner
And then I get ready for bed,
From my bedroom window
I can touch the top hat on his head.
Two buttons for his eyes and a carrot for his nose.
He is so fat and tall I'm glad he doesn't need clothes.
I'm more tired that I thought
And I sleep the morning away,
Mom comes to wake and says it's nice and warm today
I rush to the window to see where my snowman is at
But all I see is a slushy puddle with a hat.

Maggie Peikon

Charles Campagne School
Bethpage, NY
Nominated by fifth grade teacher Mrs. K. Brolly

Summer Blues

September through June,
Oh, how the months fly by.
And now that school is over,
I can't wait for July.

What to do, what to do,
I can't think of anything to play.
I've got the summer blues,
I know they'll last all day.

The sprinklers aren't working,
And I've got no pool.
How I can stand the heat,
I guess I'll never know.

The AC in my room's too warm,
The one in the den's too cold.
My brother won't come out to play,
And so I am bored.

A boring day without anyone,
A day with no fun.
And I won't admit it,
But I'm the only one.

There's one little ray of hope,
A spark of flickering light.
Tomorrow I'm going to play at the pool,
As soon as there's daylight!

My mom promised I could go on the high dive,
And on the large slide.
She said she'll take my grandma,
Just to see me dive.

My summer blues are gone,
They've all faded away.
And I just can't wait,
For my very special day.

Lisa Benenati

Charles Campagne School
Bethpage, NY
Nominated by fifth grade teacher Helen Berryman

Winter

Flakes of whirling white.
All around me,
Never stopping.
Soft coolness melting on my nose,
And cheeks.
A wall of white, blinding white.
Crunching underfoot.
Weaving patterns in the air.
Evergreens in their winter best.
The sun comes out,
It melts away,
I know it will
Come back someday.

Emma Soper

Blue Point School
Blue Point, NY
Nominated by fifth grade teacher Virginia Metzendorf

Underneath The Surface

Beneath the makeup and the skin,
Hides a wonderful girl within,
Someone who gives you her love,
Like an angel from above,
She gives you a place to go,
A place to stay,
And always knows what to say,
She shows you things you could never know,
She brings you up when you're feeling low...

Wylie Cheung

Charles Campagne School
Bethpage, NY
Nominated by fifth grade teacher Helen Berryman

Fifth Grade

I like fifth grade, I'll tell you why,
I'm learning so much, I can reach for the sky.
The math, the science, and reading too,
Will help me know whatever is new.
I'll try to learn all that I can,
So I can grow to be a smart man.

Daniel Andrew Papa

Solomon Schechter Day School
Commack, NY
Nominated by fifth grade teacher Frannie Freedman

Springtime

Flowers blooming every hour
Birds sing with dignity and with power
It seems God created spring just for me
With giant flowers and leaves on every tree
I love to listen to the bird's sweet song
I could sit and listen all day long
Their song is like music to my ears
Where everything dissolves my woes, my fears
In spring everything comes alive
The flowers bloom and the animals thrive

Megan Chadzutko

St. Mary School
East Islip, NY
Nominated by fifth grade teacher Michele Picardi

Snow

As I opened my mouth
and stuck out my tongue,
I saw the snow coming
down from the sun.

I put on my mittens
and zippered my coat,
the snow melted in my mouth
and trickled down my throat.

The taste was like
a clear mountain spring,
coming down from the sky
like no other thing.

I wanted some more
but the snow didn't fall,
so I had to sit back and savor it all.

Sarah Pattison

Dickinson Avenue School
East Northport, NY
Nominated by fifth grade teacher Liz Holbreich

The River

The river flows and nobody knows
Where it will end.
But wherever it goes,
Whether it rains or snows,
It will always be a river.
For it flows where nobody knows
Farther than where our imagination goes
Farther than where our minds will take us.

Christina Campbell

St. Mary School
East Islip, NY
Nominated by fifth grade teacher Barbara Rotkiewicz

After Dark

After dark the room stirs with silence.
I woke up and felt a cool chill go across my feet.
I fell back asleep and sunk my head into the pillow.
I dreamt dreams no one would ever.
As I lay in my bed I know I'm not the only one here.
I feel a warm breeze.
I get up and go to the window
My hair blows in my face.
I go back to bed and think a little more.
I fall asleep this time a lot quicker.
I hear the alarm clock go off.
Was that a dream? Or maybe not.

Catherine Pember

Dickinson Avenue School
East Northport, NY
Nominated by fifth grade teacher Liz Holbreich

Weather In The Fall

In the fall the leaves turn orange,
yellow and red.
In the fall the weather makes me
want to get out of my bed.
Outside my window
when the leaves fall to the ground.
I see the squirrels running
'round and 'round.
The birds are getting ready to fly south.
I like when the autumn raindrops fall
into my mouth.
In the fall the weather is really great.
In the fall kids go to school
and I am going to be late.

Rachel Stauffer

Ruth C. Kinney School
Islip Terrace, NY
Nominated by fifth grade teacher Janice Laube

My Odd Day

Oh, I've had some very odd days before,
But nothing compared to this!!
Whenever I step outside the door,
An ugly witch gives me a kiss!
I go into the bathroom to find a troll,
Playing with a toilet paper roll.
I come to the kitchen to have my dinner,
And find that my mother's a worm-eating winner.
I go to my bedroom to get ready for bed,
And notice there's a snake on my head.
I run downstairs to tell my dad,
But now he's a bull, who's REALLY mad!
I go to the family room to hopefully escape,
But find my bird is wearing a Batman cape.
I wish this day would end really soon.
It finally does! I can see the moon.
But I was wrong, for what I see,
There's a hippopotamus looking straight at me.
This may not be so weird to you,
But I'm on the fifth floor in room number two.
I turn over in my bed, and scream and shriek.
There's a polar bear giving me a peek.
A toucan bird is flying above my head,
And finally drops onto the bed.
I fall asleep to the sound of my dog,

Snoring to the thump of a dancing hog.
When I wake up, it's picture time.
My mother says, "Oh please don't whine!"
But I have NEVER had to pose
With a bouquet of flowers up my nose!
I'm sorry to say I have to end this tale,
Because in my ear, there is a whale.
I cannot hear my own self think,
Let alone -- even wink.
Good-bye my friends, I thank you for listening.
Ouch! Now the whale is whistling!
I really wish this day would end,
I definitely need to make new friends!

Katherine Hackett

St. Patrick School
Huntington, NY
Nominated by fifth grade teacher Arlene Ekis

The Monster Under My Desk

In my classroom there are many scary things
From the homework board to the drawer
Where my teacher keeps the infractions

But the most scary thing of them all
Is the monster under my desk

I don't know how he got there
But it looks like he was made up of
All the chewing gum that was stuck under my desk

Most of the time he growls
When you flick something at his nose
One time he even tried to bite me

I am the only kid in the class
Who has a monster under his desk
You would think he is a lot of trouble
But only sometimes

He is great when we have tests,
He has the book right under me
Reading the answers aloud
Mrs. Ekis tries to get him to stop
But he doesn't!

So she takes my desk and puts it outside
Sometimes it comes as a relief
That's at least what I think at the time
Until I get the grade

It isn't so bad because usually he eats the test
But I still get the grade

The good part is that my parents don't see it
'Til report card day
When my teacher tells the grades
Then I really get it

I usually get mad at my monster
So I give him the silent treatment
But that doesn't mean he is silent

He eats any part of my desk
And doesn't even think of saying sorry
But then we become friends

That is 'til report card day!

Michael Fuschillo

St. Patrick School
Huntington, NY
Nominated by fifth grade teacher Arlene Ekis

Whisper

When the green grass will whisper,
it tells about the trees that flow when the wind blows,
and how the flowers cry when winter comes by.
And how it tells about the big blue skies --
it sounds so sweet, I could cry.

Now it's autumn the leaves will fall,
the wildlife are most busy above all.
Birds fly south, bears go to sleep.
And thank you God for bringing me!

Katie Fagerland

Ruth C. Kinney School
Islip Terrace, NY
Nominated by fifth grade teacher Janice Laube

Windows On The Lake

Windows on the lake.
Each window ready to open with love, care,
And the Holy Ghost.
Each window with a gleam and the shining of the sun.
If one opens, people celebrate all over the world,
Each soul becomes one again.
The souls replenish the rivers, seas,
And the oceans of the world.
Windows on the lake.
Each window ready to open with love, care,
And the Holy Ghost.

Kevin Prego

Cayuga School
Lake Grove, NY
Nominated by fifth grade teacher Mrs. D. Koch

First Day

Today's the first day of school.
I don't think I can go.
My stomach is a baseball.
My heart is about to blow.

My mouth is like a desert.
My eyes are blurry-bright.
My ears hear all things fuzzy.
I didn't sleep last night.

My shoes are untied.
Dirt is on my shirt.
My hair is a mess.
My big toe hurts.

My hands are hiding deep in my pants.
Will pockets stop the shake?
I wish I was just dreaming.
But nope! I'm awake.

Oh, no here comes a new kid.
Bet he's not scared like me.
He walks up to me and whispers, "Hi."
And I suddenly see.

HIS hands are in his pockets.
Dirt is on his shirt and knee.
Yes! His hands are hidden deep.
"Hi, friend," You're just like me!

Paul Purcaro

Cayuga School
Lake Grove, NY
Nominated by fifth grade teacher Mrs. D. Koch

43

Squishy Fishy

Fishy, fishy,
Oh how squishy!
Gooey and green,
How it makes such a scene.
Wet and grimy,
Oh how slimy.
If only people had a meeting
Then they'd know what they were eating.
Such a creature without a doubt,
Could only gross everyone out!
Yucky fish,
Squish, squish, squish!

Kaitlyn DiGangi

Tackan Elementary School
Nesconset, NY
Nominated by fifth grade teacher Mrs. Rhodes

Manatees

Gentle and graceful,
Can never be hateful.
They're so cute and cuddly,
They'll amaze you so suddenly,
By their beautiful colors and grace.
Their black beady eyes shine so, so bright,
It looks exactly as the light.
Little black speckles all over their face,
That probably gives them all of their grace.
Their small, gray, smooth fins,
Help them to swim.
Manatees love to eat,
Though their favorite food is kelp.
These sweet loving creatures,
Really need your help.
So, I beg you adopt a manatee,
And you'll absolutely love them,
I guarantee!

Sara Kiridly

Tackan Elementary School
Nesconset, NY
Nominated by fifth grade teacher Mrs. Rhodes

Cool Cat

There's a cool cat,
He sleeps on a mat.
He wears a backwards hat.

He has a friend pig,
Who likes to do the jig.
And has a big wig.

Pig has a sister,
With a big blister.
Some think she's a mister.

Sister has a fish,
Who eats out of a dish.
His favorite is Kanish.

Cool Cat likes to eat rats,
He's also not afraid of bats.
That's unusual for cats.

This cat's really funny,
He has a wife named Bunny.
He calls her Honey.

Cool Cat doesn't like the pool,
But he loves to go to school.
This cat's really cool!

Dan Kalata and Frank Piccirillo

Tackan Elementary School
Nesconset, NY
Nominated by fifth grade teacher Mrs. Rhodes

D.A.R.E.

I have a lot of fun in D.A.R.E.
It has helped me to become aware
Of all the bad things
There are out there.

It teaches me how to say "No"
Instead of getting high
I'll stay nice and mellow.

It has helped me learn as I grow
To go out there and stay drug free
Just like D.A.R.E. has taught me.

Charlene Busuttil

Holy Angels Regional School
Patchogue, NY
Nominated by fifth grade teacher Mrs. Hammond

D.A.R.E.

Officer Neumann is very cool
She comes to our school
And teaches us not to be a fool
She has personality plus
And she passes it on to us
She works hard
To teach us right from wrong
So we can grow up
To be wise and strong
She is a lifelong friend
And her dedication will never end
Her smile is as long as a mile
And will last forever
And never fade away
Her self-esteem is as high as a beam
And she fills us with gleam
She gives us good information concerning our life
So we won't be filled with constant strife
Officer Neumann always makes the classes fun
In my opinion, she is number one!!!!!

Rebecca K. Finocchiaro

Holy Angels Regional School
Patchogue, NY
Nominated by fifth grade teacher JoAnn Tomasino

The Millennium

5, 4, 3, 2, 1
We all cheer because
The millennium has just begun
What's going to happen?
Will we ever know?

Maybe we will in space,
But for now let time keep its pace
What clothes are we going to wear?
Matching clothes so we'll look like a pair?

5, 4, 3, 2, 1
We all cheer because
The millennium has just begun
What's going to happen?
Will we ever know?

What foods are we going to eat?
Maybe food that will put us in a good mood
What sports are we going to play?
Maybe a new sport every day?

5, 4, 3, 2, 1
We all cheer because
The millennium has just begun

What's going to happen?
Will we ever know?

Hey, what about Y2K?
No electrical power?
What will happen at that hour?

5, 4, 3, 2, 1
We all cheer because
The millennium has just begun
What's going to happen?
Will we ever know?

What words are we going to speak?
I wish I could take a peek
The millennium sounds like fun
But what if it is a sign
That means soon everything will be done?

5, 4, 3, 2, 1
We all cheer because
The millennium has just begun
What's going to happen?
Will we ever know?
Now I know the answer to that question,
Nobody will know
Because anything is possible.

Marie M. Danieli

South Grove Elementary School
Syosset, NY
Nominated by fifth grade teacher June D'Amato

Rainy Day

Nothing to do
Nothing to play
All because it is a rainy day

The sky is gray
Please sun come out so we can play
I can't stay inside another day

Oh look,
Oh my,
The rain has stopped
There is no gray
Now we can go out to play!

Lisa Anne Finger

South Grove Elementary School
Syosset, NY
Nominated by fifth grade teacher June D'Amato

Valentine's Day

Today is Valentine's Day
People go out of their way on Valentine's Day
They hug, they kiss, hey what's this!
People go out of their way on Valentine's Day

Cookies, chocolate, and candy
Everyone is dandy
People go out of their way on Valentine's Day
Presents and more
This is galore
People go out of their way on Valentine's Day

Today is Valentine's Day
People are loving and nice
As sugar and spice
People go out of their way on Valentine's Day

Kristyn Marie Lang

South Grove Elementary School
Syosset, NY
Nominated by fifth grade teacher June D'Amato

The River

The river glimmers
like
a shiny metal
made
of silver.

The current
flows
strong but smooth.

It carves out
crumbling mountains
with its power.

It flows
soft as silk.

The river
splashes, splashes, splashes
as it flows.

Steven Pockels

Village Elementary School
Syosset, NY
Nominated by fifth grade teacher Ms. Potenzone

Spring

Luscious fruit trees
Dancing in a gentle breeze
A waterfall so high
Roaring as it rushes by
The green meadows with flowers so bright
Warming themselves by the sunlight
The sky so blue
Speckled with white fluff too
The harmony of spring
We all sing

Ruti Gerstel

Torah Academy for Girls
Far Rockaway, NY
Nominated by fifth grade teacher Liorah Rachwarger

Grandpa

The wind whistling like a faraway train
the crisp dead leaves
touch my glamorous shoes and skirt
I hear everybody talking and whispering
I walk into the funeral
too silent for words
just right for tears
it's hot and stuffy in there
I pray on the cushion next to him
I take one glance
just one glance at him
I flew out of the hot stuffy room
to me everything looked like it was crying
the blazing sun
the whistling wind
the crunchy dead leaves
that was a very
miserable
depressing day

My heart melting
in the pot of my sadness
I stand there
waiting
dreaming
this isn't
happening

Debbie Citarella

Village Elementary School
Syosset, NY
Nominated by fifth grade teacher Ms. McEvoy

A Dream Come True

Some memories at the beach
I remember

The glimmering white sand
tickling your toes

The glistening ray of the sun's heat
beating upon your head

Let the calm cool waves
float away your troubles

Listen to all the excitement
of kids enjoying themselves in the sand

The big giants
in front of me are my mom,
dad and nana

My mom's hair straight as a board
down to her shoulders
with her tiny little diamond earrings
sparkling wherever she goes
with her big smile
up to her ears

my mom picking me up
and humming to me
always put me asleep

My dad's sandals
bigger than my head
with his calming voice
that always soothed me

My nana's hair
just like a puffy gray cloud in the sky
her eyes blue as the ocean
her voice saying
look how cute
always comforted me

I lay down in my tent
and all the sounds made me relaxed

Erich Stingelin

Village Elementary School
Syosset, NY
Nominated by fifth grade teacher Ms. McEvoy

Season Of Winter

Winter is coming,
The cold weather's here;
Here's the first snowfall,
Very, very near;
I like the icy weather,
I don't mind the cold,
The only thing I don't like,
My grandpa died when he was old;
Otherwise I'm happy,
And it's very, very fun,
So say good-bye to the summer,
And the bright bright sun.

It's my second favorite season,
Besides the hot hot summer,
I know someone else who likes it,
The very happy drummer;
People don't like winter,
I don't know why,
People only like it,
When the temperature's very high,
Only the drummer and I like it,
That is only two people,
Some people say,
Winter is very very evil.

Snowmen, snow angels, and snowballs,
Are all in this season,
Lots of people trying to call Sears,
To get their heaters heatin';
All those people who say winter's bad,
All of them are wrong,
It's a season of joy,
And Christmas song!
But all of that fun stuff is done,
Like swimming, parties, and the beach,
And now we go to school,
And hear the teacher teach.

Jon Pantazi

Leonard E. Burket Christian School
Center Moriches, NY
Nominated by fifth grade teacher Ruth Burket

The Christmas Tree

I am a tree not just a regular tree,
but a Christmas tree.
I'm a special tree that gets decorated
with love and memories.
But after December 25th, I get packed away
not to return 'til the next year.
I'm so lonely in my box packed so far away.
So dusty and old my box is
but the only thing I can think of is being a symbol.
A symbol of Christ next year at Christmas.
All the Christmas carols gone.
I wish I had a friend to be near.
I still have memories of last Christmas to comfort me.
I count the days one by one for that very special one.
Christmas Day.
After three hundred and sixty-five days alone
they finally opened the box and took me out.
I was so excited and happy
they put me in a stand
and started to put ornaments on me.
I couldn't believe my eyes, I looked beautiful.

And I could hear the Christmas carols.
I was so happy.
But the thing that brought the most joy,
was being used as a symbol.
A symbol of Christ's birth.
Christ the ruler of all creation.

Kelly Nicole Leonard

Leonard E. Burket Christian School
Center Moriches, NY
Nominated by fifth grade teacher Ruth Burket

Sunrise

First it's dark
Then it's pink
Then it's light
Then it's sunrise
Then it's dawn
Morning dew
Against my feet
Tall green grass
Scratch my legs
Warm summer day.

Alicia Obler

The Ross School
East Hampton, NY
Nominated by fifth grade teacher Barbara Raeder-Tracy

As A Friend

If you were my enemy
I would not do a thing with you.
I would stay as far away as I could get from you
and never speak to you.

But you are my friend, so I like to play,
laugh and sing with you.
We will always be friends forever,
never enemies.

Larissa Gaias

The Ross School
East Hampton, NY
Nominated by fifth grade teacher Barbara Raeder-Tracy

Blue

Blue is the color of sadness
It makes me want to cry
It always brings my head low
and I let out a great sigh.

Blue is that one blue jay
that loves to fly and fly,
he flies around on sunny days
when rain comes I say bye-bye.

Blue is the color of that car
that rides up and down my street
The car goes so fast
it's off the block in one heartbeat.

Stefanie Dovak

Moriches Elementary School
Moriches, NY
Nominated by fifth grade teacher Susan Gleason

Green is the color of the trees.
Green is more than what is seems.

Leprechauns dance in the green, green grass.
They play all day in the clovers.

Green are the lizards who eat the plants.
Green are the rotted old pants.
Green are the pickles that are eaten by us.

Green is the perfect color to me.

Elizabeth Brower

Moriches Elementary School
Moriches, NY
Nominated by fifth grade teacher Susan Gleason

My Many Colored Days

When I think of red,
I think of warmth, happiness and love.
When I think of blue,
I think of cool water, when the sun is hot above.
When I think of gray,
It's winter and everything is mad.
When I think of purple,
I think of flowers in a dreamland.
When I think of gold,
I think of the sweet sound of a brass band.
When I think of black,
I think of being in a dark, dark room.
When I think of brown,
I think of the handle of a broom.
When I think of yellow,
I think of wildflowers in a meadow.
When I think of white,
I think of the cream inside of an Oreo.
My many colored days will never end.

Patricia Marshall

John S. Hobart Elementary School
Shirley, NY
Nominated by fifth grade teacher Dolores Stiles

Mysterious Animals Of The Sea

Something lives under the sea,
And it's quite a sight for you and me.

It can be spongy, hard, big or small,
With names like Grooved Brain,
Yellow Pencil and Golfball.

It can be food for some fish,
And a home for some too.
They come in different colors
Such as red, white and blue.

It's amazing beyond belief,
It's a colorful coral reef!

Matthew Liguori

Ridge Elementary School
Ridge, NY
Nominated by fifth grade teacher Barbara Schaer

I Looked Out My Window

I looked out my window
I saw a monkey in a tree
I saw a horse and a honeybee
I saw a meadow and a fawn
I saw a frog on my lawn
I saw a dragonfly by a waterfall
I saw the sunset over them all
I saw the moon white and round
I saw the stars looking down

Alyse N. Gandalone

Ridge Elementary School
Ridge, NY
Nominated by fifth grade teacher Hughette Clarke

Clock

Tick, tick, tick,
tock, tock, tock,
this sound comes,
from my clock.
Beep, beep, beep,
this comes next,
waking me from
my long rest.
I sit up with an awful yawn,
look out my window,
to see a fawn.
It has been,
awakened too,
just like me,
and just like you!

Jacky Haase

Southold Elementary School
Southold, NY
Nominated by fifth grade teacher Donna Laymon

Colors

Orange makes me feel warm,
like being by a campfire.

Yellow makes me feel cheerful,
like hiking in the woods on a sunny day.

Blue reminds me of being at the beach
and feeling the cool breeze, giving me a chill.

Black reminds me of when I am all alone in my bed
sitting in the dark of night.

Red makes me mad, like a burning hot fire
from a fireplace in the winter.

Light pink makes me feel alone and far away,
like in the open country sitting on a rocking chair
humming a soft tune.

Green reminds me of many gardens with vegetables
like peas and zucchini.

Purple makes me confused, like knowing something,
but forgetting it.

Brown makes me feel strong,
like playing a game and doing my best.

Gray makes me feel crummy, like sitting by the window
and watching the rain come down.

And lastly, white reminds me of the light, soft snow
falling on the ground on Christmas morning.

Lauren Vernice

John S. Hobart Elementary School
Shirley, NY
Nominated by fifth grade teacher Nina Mittman

Rain And Shine

Drip drop
Plip plop
Hear the rain come pouring down
Splashing as it hits the ground
The weather is stormy
Puddles are forming
In the car it's really boring
I cannot stand these cloudy skies
I think I just might close my eyes
Wait! What's this I see?
Can it actually be the sun shining through the trees?
Thank goodness the sun has finally come out
Now let's just hope there isn't a drought

Nicole Sinning

Southold Elementary School
Southold, NY
Nominated by fifth grade teacher Donna Laymon

Standing On Top

I stand on top of a mountain
and see what is below me.

I see the small mountains,
they look as tiny as a leaf
at the very top of a tree.

I hear the wind
making a ch-ch-ch sound
through the trees.

I feel like I am on top of the world.
I can see everything.
I can hear everything.
I can feel everything.

Maria Simone

Wheelerville School
Caroga Lake, NY
Nominated by fifth grade teacher Francis J. Kwiatkowski

Play Ball

The snow is gone, the spring is here.
The team is ready, excitement is in the air.
The umpire calls "Play ball."
The game is on,
The pitcher throws, the batter swings,
The umpire calls "STRIKE ONE."
The ball is pitched a second time,
"STRIKE TWO!"
The batter gets ready,
The ball goes over the plate -- "CRACK"
The catcher throws off his mask,
The umpire yells "Home run!"
The game is over, my team won!

Connor Wager

Wheelerville School
Caroga Lake, NY
Nominated by fifth grade teacher Francis J. Kwiatkowski

Mission To Mars

5,4,3,2,1 Liftoff goes the rocket
Halfway in space a bolt falls out of its socket!
The fuel tank falls! The thrusters go out!
We have little luck or we might be out.
Halfway to Mars something went wrong.
I put on my suit and went to see what's going on!
A comet came by and just missed my head!
If that hit me, I would be dead!
When we were on Mars,
We were taken by a dust tornado!
The dirt there feels like Play-Doh?!
One hour later my air tank explodes!
Back to the ship I had to go.
Back in space we will roam.
Eventually we will get home.
This mission to Mars went terribly wrong.
That's why we were gone so long.

Andrew P. Lakata

Wheelerville School
Caroga Lake, NY
Nominated by fifth grade teacher Francis J. Kwiatkowski

The Girl

There once was a girl of old,
Whose hair was spun of gold.
She was not adored,
In fact she was ignored
As she spoke to all too bold..

Taryn Cooper

Mayfield Elementary School
Mayfield, NY
Nominated by fifth grade teacher Tara Yager

The Lion

There once was a mean old lion,
and everyone kept on tryin',
to tame the beast,
but the lion had a feast.
Now who's doin' all the cryin'?

Jared Jones

Mayfield Elementary School
Mayfield, NY
Nominated by fifth grade teacher Tara Yager

A Cat Named Rover

There once was a fat, lazy cat.
It walked out to the road and just sat.
The cat was named Rover,
A car ran him over.
And now the fat cat was flat.

Kimberly Negrich

Mayfield Elementary School
Mayfield, NY
Nominated by fifth grade teacher Tara Yager

Funny The Way My Family Can Be

Funny the way,
my family can be,
Mom vacuums the house every Sunday,
Dad sleeps on the couch after working on Monday,
sister is always a pain,
Grandma always has time to explain,
cousins live far away,
friends come over to play,
Grandpa feeds the dog a biscuit,
my aunt finds time to knit,
Uncles usually watching sports,
and I'm sometimes on basketball courts,
and it's funny the way,
my family can be.

Ryne Barber

Mayfield Elementary School
Mayfield, NY
Nominated by fifth grade teacher Faye DeLilli

Upside-Down World

As I hang from my bed,
Standing on my head,
I enter the upside-down world.

With lights on the floor,
And the kitty I adore
Hanging calmly from the ceiling by her toes.

When my mother walks in,
She doesn't notice a thing!
But walks back across the ceiling to the door.

It seems strange to see,
Everyone upside down but me
As if I'm not even there at all.

Then CRASH! BOOM! BASH!
And one big CLASH!
I'm back in the regular world.

'Til I'm back on my head,
Visiting again.
Back in the upside-down world.

Emily Staats

Vann Rensselaer School
Rensselaer, NY
Nominated by fifth grade teacher Cristine Lonnstrom

A Mystical Ocean

A mystical wonderful place.
A gentle light touches my face.
Mermaids with glittering hair,
Float by like clouds in the air.

Sarah Angela Jevons

Vann Rensselaer School
Rensselaer, NY
Nominated by fifth grade teacher Mrs. Weir

Forever

Forever they love,
Forever they cherish.
The beauty of life,
The smiles of faces.
Forever life flows through
The good and the bad.
To make us happy with life in our hearts.

Caitlin Elacqua

St. Jude the Apostle School •
Wynantskill, NY
Nominated by fifth grade teacher Mrs. DeGraff

Sunny Side Bay

At Sunny Side Bay, there's much to do,
like play in the dirt, and collect snail shells too!
There're dogs running around having their fun,
and people taking tans in the sun.
There're kids flying kites in the sky,
they reach way up where the airplanes fly.
There's a big oak tree, and stumps lying around,
and moss in some spots covers the ground.
There's also an ice-cream stand owned by Mr. Best.
He makes the best ice cream miles above the rest.
His stand is seated where the garden has been hoed.
He serves vanilla, chocolate, strawberry,
and rocky road.
Speaking about the garden, it's a marvelous site.
The flowers are all different colors, shapes,
and heights.
As the sun starts to set, we start to settle down.
We'd never leave this place, on our faces a frown.
It's another sunny day,
at the Sunny Side Bay.

Alicia Marie Cruickshank

St. Jude the Apostle School
Wynantskill, NY
Nominated by fifth grade teacher Mrs. DeGraff

Flying

I wish I could fly
High in the sky
All around the world.
Snow-covered mountains,
Rain showers like fountains
Sunset, sunrise,
Everywhere a surprise.
How lovely would that be.
All the great things I could see.

Michelle Geisler

Hebrew Academy
Albany, NY
Nominated by fifth grade teacher Hilary Anapolsky

Princess

I know a princess named Lily,
Who lives in the country of Italy.
When I see her, I think of my kitty
For they both are very pretty.

Oh Lily, oh Lily, my brother likes you
Every day he sees you at school.
But everyone thinks he is a fool,
Because of how he feels about you.

Sara Gasorowski

Public School # 20
Albany, NY
Nominated by fifth grade teacher Virginia Terrell

87

Music, Music

Music, music in the air,
music playin' everywhere,
music that fills my heart delight,
music playin' every night,
music on the saxophone,
music that makes me want to dance on home,
music on the clarinet,
music that will make me jump up yet,
music playin' through my head,
music before I go to bed...

Peter Rowell

Sacandaga School
Scotia, NY
Nominated by fifth grade teacher Carol Glindmyer

We are trapped in this
World of hatred and anger,
With no place to go,
We suffer from our own cause,
Wilting little by little is our earth,
Wilting little by little are our souls,
Worthlessly we destroy ourselves along
With everything around us,
When we do this to our once
Wonderfully Utopian earth,
We're not helping anything,
Well I have one question,

WHY?

I pray that one day peace,
Will overcome all the
Wondrous lands
We will all be equal
There will be righteousness everywhere
Our earth will stop wilting
Will bloom vibrantly,
Our souls will sprout with joy,
It will be...

UTOPIA

Cagney Houlihan

Sacandaga School
Scotia, NY
Nominated by fifth grade teacher Carol Glindmyer

Who Am I?

I work hard night and day,
With very little or no pay,
My family goes without food and clothes,
I own no shoes for my toes,
I have no freedom.
My name is Dave.
As you can read.
I am a SLAVE.

Bryan R. Van Wagenen

Riccardi Elementary School
Saugerties, NY
Nominated by fifth grade teacher Mr. R. Speirs

Summertime

At summertime the flowers bloom,
The animals sing a happy tune.
There're daisies, lilacs, and pansies too.
Satin pinks and crimson reds,
Are roses in my flower bed.
Delightful fragrance fills the air,
Just waiting to be picked and shared.
Today, we found some yellow buds,
The sun gave us its latest loves.
Oh joy! What happy days ahead,
All found right here in my flower bed.

Nicole Richardson

Riccardi Elementary School
Saugerties, NY
Nominated by fifth grade teacher Diana Voerg

Utopia

Where candy grows on trees,
and laughter fills the air,
ice-cream clouds dance through the sky,
a breeze blows back your hair...

The sun kisses you with warmth,
the cool shade licks your nose,
tall grass tickles you as it sways,
all around you, the aroma of a rose...

Where nighttime fires crackle,
and clothing's made of silk,
people do not go hungry,
mountains are pizza, and rivers, milk...

As you walk into a crystal-blue lake,
water surrounds you, no need for clothes,
dunk your head under, hair floating freely,
squeeze the sand with your toes...

Leisurely floating atop the water,
a soft wind whispers in your ear,
"This place is filled with peace and harmony."
...all happiness... no fear.

Desirae Clark

Sacandaga School
Scotia, NY
Nominated by fifth grade teacher Carol Glindmyer

I Wish

My hard day's work has finally ended,
My master's clothes are completely mended.
While the children catch fireflies,
I sit on the stump by the riverbank
And wish on the bright shining stars
in the moonlit sky
I wish on one and say,
"I wish to die or to be freed today!"

Caitlin Virginia Turk

Riccardi Elementary School
Saugerties, NY
Nominated by fifth grade teacher Diana Voerg

Invitation

Come with me to a beautiful forest
where the animals are made of silk
and shimmer in the sun.

Come with me to a place
where diamonds grow on the edges of leaves
and sway while the wind will blow.

Come with me to a place of love
where everyone is happy all up above.

Amanda Whalen

Kildonan Elementary School
Amenia, NY
Nominated by fifth grade teacher Christina Lund

Invitation

You are invited to:

The American Civil War
from 1861-1865

(The Civil War is a field of gore.)

Bring a pistol, alcohol and playing cards.
Wear a Union Civil War uniform.

(The Civil War is a field of gore.)

Games will include: cannonball targeting,
hostage tag and races to see who can slice
the most watermelons while on a horse.

(The Civil War is a field of gore.)

Please R.S.V.P   24, Civil Drive,
                              Gettysburg Lane,
                              Pennsylvania
                              America.

Brian J. Nemlich

Kildonan Elementary School
Amenia, NY
Nominated by fifth grade teacher Christina Lund

If You Were Here...

Grandpa, if you were here...
I would watch Jeopardy with you tonight.
You would answer all the questions and say,
"I'd give YOU that $500 Jonah."

Grandpa, if only you were here tonight...
We would go to the market
and get fresh pastries and strawberries
and eat them while we play croquet.
I can just see you grinning as you beat me
saying, "I beat you this time,
but you'll probably beat me next time."

Grandpa, if only I could call you with Bell Atlantic
and we could talk about World War II.
You could tell me about how you fought in the war.

Life and death are like being in jail
talking over a phone with bars between us,
between heaven and earth.

You are here, but you're not here.

Jonah Grumbine

Kildonan Elementary School
Amenia, NY
Nominated by fifth grade teacher Christina Lund

96

The white herons flew
Over the vast blue ocean
Around the splashing whales
Behind the flipping dolphins
Across many islands
They flew far and wide
High and low
The herons flew to daybreak
But, now they fly no more.

Kate Centrowitz

Cornwall Elementary School
Cornwall, NY
Nominated by fifth grade teacher Linda S. Auerbach

What Do You See?

Look up in the sky, what do you see?
Shining stars, as bright as can be.
Look down to the ground, what do you see?
Thick blades of grass, as green as can be.
Look out at the ocean, what do you see?
Whitecapped waves, as big as can be.
Look into the forest, what do you see?
Scurrying creatures, as frightened as can be.
Look into the mirror, what do you see?
A reflection so beautiful, and fragile as can be.

Elizabeth Michele Piggott

North Park Elementary School
Hyde Park, NY
Nominated by fifth grade teacher Felicia Olson

Animals

I have a dog at home
and he is a hog.
He may be tall
but we have a ball.

I have a cat
and she is a brat.
I like to pat the cat,
sometimes she looks like a mat.

I wish I had a horse
of course it would be a lot of work
but it would be worth it
I could use the work.

There is a tiger in my yard
he is bigger than my St. Bernard
I shiver when I see him
he needs to go back to the zoo.

I have a hamster
who likes to be a dancer
sometimes she prances on my toes
so I call her Twinkle Toes.

Terri Hart

North Park Elementary School
Hyde Park, NY
Nominated by fifth grade teacher Felicia Olson

Flowers

They're all different colors
and can be found up and down the streets.
They're planted in gardens and smell so sweet.
When you are coming up and down the street
you'll see something beautiful and also sweet
they are flowers.
They make you happy when you are sad.
Flowers they'll always keep you feeling glad.

Chelsea Thorpe

North Park Elementary School
Hyde Park, NY
Nominated by fifth grade teacher Felicia Olson

Blue

Blue is the color of my elbow pad
My elbow pad protects my elbow
My elbow pad was a gift to me
I am a gift to my mother
My mother is a gift from God

Nicholas Digilio

New Windsor School
New Windsor, NY
Nominated by fifth grade teacher Ilene Rabinowe

Responsibility

It's my Responsibility to be all I can be.
Oh it's my Responsibility to try
and be Responsible.
If I couldn't be Responsible
I don't know what I would do.
The way to be Responsible
is to just put your mind to it.
Responsibility is sometimes fun
but don't try to take advantage.
Listen to the few words I say
and try to be Responsible.

Tonia King

Broadway School
Newburgh, NY
Nominated by fifth grade teacher Christine Countryman

My New Teacher

I have a new teacher
tomorrow she'll come.
I am quite nervous
my fingers are numb.
I got her some flowers,
some pink candy hearts,
a diamond necklace,
a dress that is dandy.
I got her a vase
and a gold-plated fan.
Then I found out,
my new teacher's a man!

Jessica Lynn Marshall

New Windsor School
New Windsor, NY
Nominated by fifth grade teacher Ellen Rones

Outside Inside

Outside the moon creeps up.
Inside I lay still under my covers.
Outside the hail pounding at the roof awakens me.
Inside I sit up silently in my bed.
Outside shooting stars bolt across the black sky.
Inside I now watch the night stars.
Outside the moon peeks
from the dark snow clouds soon to open.
Inside I watch small flurries drift onto my window sill.
Outside the clouds open and the blizzard starts.
The hail stops.
Inside I now go to bed under my nice warm covers.

Christina Hoffman

Myers Corners School
Wappingers Falls, NY
Nominated by fifth grade teacher Dianne Foxhall

Spring Senses

The sun is bright,
The clouds are white,
I have sight.

The air smells sweet,
Like a strawberry-covered treat,
I have smell.

I taste the nectar,
It's more than splendor,
I have taste.

I touch the tree,
Then a soft little bee,
I have touch.

I hear the grasshoppers' chime,
Like the dropping of a dime,
I can hear.

Natasha Crawford

St. Peter's School
Poughkeepsie, NY
Nominated by fifth grade teacher Mrs. Wynne

My Dog Tina

My dog Tina now is dead,
but memories of her still live on in my head.
The times we played catch in the park,
the times we were sleeping alone in the dark.
One memory I can't seem to forget
is when I saw that needle go into her leg,
that painful sight, it gave me such a fright.
I didn't know what to do,
I just cried oh no this can't be true.

Shauna Rudden

St. Peter's School
Poughkeepsie, NY
Nominated by fifth grade teacher Mrs. Wynne

The Land Of The Free
And The Home Of The Brave

I wish I was the land of the free
And the home of the brave.
Then I could feed the hungry and free the slaves.
Forbidding the war and stopping the fights,
Taking citizens out of darkness, putting them in light.
If I were the land of the free and the home of the brave,
Bet your bottom dollar everything would change.

Consuela Jones

Krieger School
Poughkeepsie, NY
Nominated by fifth grade teacher Diane Gleichenhaus

Baseball

When the winter is done
We look forward to spring fun
With a longer day
We look forward to May

In spring we start to play ball
Running hard, trying not to fall
Practice all long day
Practice will have to pay

Hitting, running, sliding
The second basemen not abiding
When you cross home plate
You will be greeted by your teammate

Standing at home plate with the bat
I hope the ball goes over his hat
When the ball goes over the fence
The applause will be immense.

Michael Ladonne

Anna S. Kuhl School
Port Jervis, NY
Nominated by fifth grade teacher Mrs. N. Cacchione

Music

Music is what I like --
Even on my dirt bike.
I listen day and night
Even with my friend Mike.

I listen all the time
Even if it doesn't rhyme.
If it's a crime --
I'll do my time.

I listen in my bed
Playing N64
When my mom thinks I'm done
I listen a little more.

Music is so much fun
It makes me want to scream
But when I'm done
I just dream, dream, dream.

Robert Tangen

Anna S. Kuhl School
Port Jervis, NY
Nominated by fifth grade teacher Mrs. N. Cacchione

Mom

Mom is as sweet as candy
She loves the beach
She loves the sand
Her favorite fruit is peach.

She always is my closest friend
Ready to face the trials of life
Always had a smile on her face
Always ready for our fights.

She always is the best mom
Never yelled at us
Always made my birthday cakes just right
Never tried to burn the crust.

A mom is a special thing
You are lucky if you have one
Always saying you grew up so fast
Always ready to have fun.

Dedicated to my mother and all the others
that have dedicated their lives to children
and are there when children need them.

Kayla Bickell

Anna S. Kuhl School
Port Jervis, NY
Nominated by fifth grade teacher Mrs. N. Cacchione

Suppose!

Suppose we had no voice to speak,
mouth to talk,
air to breathe.
Suppose we had no mind to think,
ears to hear,
water to drink.
Suppose we had none of this stuff,
and if we didn't, we'd all be fluff!

Keleigh A. Williams

The King's School
Lake Luzerne, NY
Nominated by fifth grade teacher Teri Lee

I Play With Mud

No! No! No! I say don't tell anyone,
For if you do, they will surely say ew!
Don't tell, please, don't tell I play with mud.
The girls will say mud is icky, mud is wet,
Mud is icky, sticky, gooey stuff.
We hate mud, we hate mud!
It's too squishy, it's too wet,
It's too disgusting of a mess!

Tina Ganter

The King's School
Lake Luzerne, NY
Nominated by fifth grade teacher Teri Lee

Candlelight

The power's out, what to do?
Light a candle, maybe two.
It's late at night, and it's cold,
the sound of cracking trees is big and bold.
"It's an ice storm, I am told."
The candles are big and bright,
and I keep warm by the candlelight.

Emily Jeanne Murphy

St. Regis Falls Central School
St. Regis Falls, NY
Nominated by fifth grade teacher Ellen Smith

Garden Of Life

Pink and white flowers
In a garden of brightness
A garden of life

J. Brittany Amsdell

Fremont Elementary School
East Syracuse, NY
Nominated by fifth grade teachers
Diane Eubank and Colleen Austin

Wolves In The Wind

As the wind is blowing in your face
you feel it blow through your hair.
You can smell roses.
You see a butterfly as it lands in your hair.
The sun sets, the butterfly flies away.
It's a full moon you can hear wolves.
When you hear the wolves
you get up and go see where they are, you find them.
They're beautiful.
One walks over to you, it doesn't bite
it just gives a little grin, you smile back.
You go home.
The next morning when you wake up
hummingbirds are at your window.
You go for a walk you see a buck, a doe, and their fawn
drinking from a babbling brook.
You keep walking farther into the woods,
you hear whimpering you look around
you see the head wolf of the pack
the one you saw last night.
He's got his forepaw caught in a snare.
You help him out, he licks your face.
You take a walk that night after he's free and you see him,
he gives you the grin again -- and you smile.

Hilary McLaughlin

St. Regis Falls Central School
St. Regis Falls, NY
Nominated by fifth grade teacher Ellen Smith

Insects

Insects
small, annoying
chirps, bites, squirms
rushing around the air
Bugs

Michelle Riedman

Fremont Elementary School
East Syracuse, NY
Nominated by fifth grade teacher Joan Vivelo

Nicole Nelson

Nice, loving, funny
Daughter of John
Wishes to have a good life
Dreams of going to Harvard
Wants to live in a mansion
Who wonders if UFO's are real
Who fears of falling off a bridge
Who is afraid of spiders
Who likes dancing
Who believes in stopping pollution
Who loves singing, dancing and playing sports
Who plans to have a good job,
Get married and have children
A GREAT FRIEND

Nicole Nelson

Fremont Elementary School
East Syracuse, NY
Nominated by fifth grade teacher Julie Bourke

The Fish

My biggest fish was big and round
A bigger fish I have not found.
It pulled and pulled so many times
I thought it just might break my line.

It almost pulled me in the water.
I thought that I had hooked an otter.
Then I started fighting back
I was pretty sure I had hooked a jack.

Finally he broke my line.
My friend said, "Better luck next time."
That fish would have been good to cook.
He might have been one for the record book.

Matthew A. Sears

Homer Intermediate School
Homer, NY
Nominated by fifth grade teacher Rod Comolli

A Pencil's Life

Hi, I'm #2 and I'm a pencil
You can use me to write, or trace off a stencil.
I like #1's, but I hate pens,
Other utensils are not my friends.
It hurts when people sharpen me,
And when they write, I cannot see.
The life of a pencil is not easy,
But a lot of people think it's breezy.

Rachel Kotlove

Homer Intermediate School
Homer, NY
Nominated by fifth grade teacher Rod Comolli

Daisy And Maisy

There once was a little cat,
Who was really rather fat.
She only lay on her mat,
And that made it awful flat.

Her name was Daisy,
She had a friend Maisy.
Boy were they lazy,
And sometimes they acted a little crazy.

They would try to snatch all the food to eat,
When they played they would bite people's feet.
They curled up on people's seats,
Then they would beg and beg for treats.

One day they met up with a tiny mouse,
Chasing it around the house.
It was such a funny sight,
Watching them run and fight.

They never acted very tired,
But they were really wound and wired.
Then one day the mouse got mean,
Disappeared and was not seen.

UNTIL...
He snuck up and bit the cats' tails,
And you could really hear their wails.
Now they were sent to kitty jail,
And they were looking pretty pale.

The lesson is an easy one,
Remember you need to have some fun.
But it's not only tit for tat,
So please don't forget that!!!!!!!

Stephanie Battista

Charles E. Riley Elementary School
Oswego, NY
Nominated by fifth grade teacher Linda Goewey

My Dreams

When I dream it's usually good,
Because I dream of happiness when I could.
I would fall into a trance,
Maybe dream I'm in France.
Make pictures in my mind,
Or even shapes and lines.

My dreams are exciting,
Even describing.
My dreams are fun,
And never done.

Dreams, dreams come and go,
Just like a tornado.
My dreams are like a sunny day,
Bright and shining, like in May.

I daydream every chance I get,
I drift away like a jet.
Dreams bring you joy,
Like playing with a favorite toy.

Do you wish? Do you hope?
I'd sure be happy if you didn't say, "Nope"
But if you did it's all right with me,
Because you always have fantasies.

Alicia Canale

Charles E. Riley Elementary School
Oswego, NY
Nominated by fifth grade teacher Linda Goewey

Blue Sky

Blue sky, blue sky
Another blue sky over the mountain high.
Over there you can see
Near the big old apple tree.
Don't you marvel over there,
Near the wondrous beautiful air.
It's meant to be for you,
And for me.

Laura E. Mantelli

St. Mary's School
Waterloo, NY
Nominated by fifth grade teacher Tammy Hoadley

I Love The Lord Jesus Christ

I love the Lord Jesus Christ,
Because he made such a big sacrifice.
I do something every day,
That thing is that I pray.
Once or twice is just fine,
Because he is so divine.
Jesus Christ loves us all,
People that are short and people that are tall.
In his eyes we are all the same,
Even if people think we are lame.
If you believe in Jesus Christ,
You will have eternal life.

Erika Jay Smith

St. Mary's School
Waterloo, NY
Nominated by fifth grade teacher Tammy Hoadley

Tiger In The Night

In the forest of the night,
lies a white tiger burning up the night.
It goes from here to there lighting up everywhere.
Somewhere in the forest of the night,
lies another tiger brightening up the night.
You cannot find them here or there,
lighting up anywhere.
You could see them if you dare
to go into the forest anywhere,
but beware!

Nicholas Batson

St. Mary's School
Waterloo, NY
Nominated by fifth grade teacher Tammy Hoadley

Seventh Grade

I dislike it -- it's too hard
I don't know if I can make it
Will I fail?
Will it hail?
I don't know!

Get a bucket full of water
Pour it over me!

Can I make it?
Can I take it?
Will I faint before I make it?
Or will I die with all this homework?
Tell me now before I cry!

Jessica Ariola

Living Word Academy
Syracuse, NY
Nominated by fifth grade teacher Jennifer Connor

Where The Mermaids Live

Way deep down where the mermaids live
They play and swim and take and give
And when they come to a stone cold cave
They know they must behave
This is where buried treasure lies
Far away from human eyes.

The mermaids go to their mermaid schools
And then come home to their mermaid pools
When they come to their shipwrecked homes
They might find a pearl in their oyster shell stones
It will be quite a sight
For this pearl they will find
Only once in their lifetime.

Nicole Anne Romano

Living Word Academy
Syracuse, NY
Nominated by fifth grade teacher Jennifer Connor

Important People

I am sad almost in tears
like a stream running down my face
thinking of you
you changed my train of thought
you inspired me
no confusion
nothing at all
you made me feel wonderful
you showed me what caring is

Sydney Andrina Moreau

Roberts Elementary School
Syracuse, NY
Nominated by fifth grade teacher Diane Brisson

I Am Me

I am me
shy, kind, artistic.
I can be sad
lonely, confused, depressed.

I am me
funny, sleepy, smart.
I can be happy
cheerful, excited, delighted.

I am NOT you!
You may be sad.
You are not me
lonely, confused, depressed.

I am NOT you!
You may be happy.
You're not me
cheerful, excited, delighted.

I am like a caterpillar,
I am changing.
Not to a butterfly
to a better me!

I am like a bee.
I am busy.
Not gathering pollen,
gathering knowledge.

I am me.
Not a caterpillar or a bee.
I am not you.
I am me.

I like me
shy, quiet, kind, me.
I like me
smart cheerful, confused, me.

I like me a lot
because it's who I am.

Erin Harding

Roberts Elementary School
Syracuse, NY
Nominated by fifth grade teacher Diane Brisson

The Ocean

I sit under the star-packed sky.
The moon shines bright
As the slow tide comes in
Stretching to the top of the sand.

The quiet song of the waves
Makes the starfish dance
As the light of the pale moon
Shines across the water.

As I lie there, smelling the salty air,
Nighttime fades and the moon goes down
Little by little.
The stars fade with it.

A curtain of purples and deep pinks
Lies over the ocean
As the sun makes her entrance
And the dolphins greet the new day.

April Ventura

Most Holy Rosary School
Syracuse, NY
Nominated by fifth grade teacher
Sister Catherine Anthony

The Color Yellow

I am confused and embarrassed.
It was Bright Yellow Day at school.
I wore yellow to school.
All of my friends wore dark purple.

I feel like a fool.
I am so confused and embarrassed.
I am sweating.
My cheeks are like a red pepper.
I feel like a track runner.
I am sweating trying to reach my goal.
My heart sounds like elephants
running through the street.

I was right
My friends were wrong.
The color of the day was truly
YELLOW!

Kristi Sprague

Roberts Elementary School
Syracuse, NY
Nominated by fifth grade teacher Diane Brisson

Tears

When I first got sad,
it felt like the whole world went bad.
My sunny day just turned upside down,
the smile on my circus clown now looks like a frown.
There's nothing really to smile about,
all I can do is sit here and pout.
As I sit here and cry I wonder why,
why did this happen to me?
It's like I got locked out of my heart,
and lost the key.

Tricia Juiliani

Most Holy Rosary School
Syracuse, NY
Nominated by fifth grade teacher
Sister Catherine Anthony

Snow leopard
beautiful fur
has binocular vision
loves fresh deer meat
Endangered

William Cain

St. Rose of Lima School
North Syracuse, NY
Nominated by fifth grade teacher
Kathleen C. Giannandrea

Why?

Why is the grass so green?
Why is it that when anyone gets mad they are mean?
Why is the sky so blue?
Why is it that you don't listen when I talk to you?

Why is school the best place to learn?
Why do we have to wait to take a turn?
Why are inventions so important to us?
Why can't I drive the car instead of the bus?

Why do people always have to be so sad?
Why do people always have to be so mad?
I don't understand these questioning laws,
Why?... Simply because.

Meredith Mosley

St. Rose of Lima School
North Syracuse, NY
Nominated by fifth grade teacher
Kathleen C. Giannandrea

Rainbows

God made them for us
They are very beautiful
Symbol of God's love

AnneMarie Giannandrea

St. Rose of Lima School
North Syracuse, NY
Nominated by fifth grade teacher
Kathleen C. Giannandrea

First Place Prize

At our annual school science fair,
I was so nervous I was plucking out my hair.
The judges were at the exhibit next to me,
It was going to win I could clearly see.
Finally the judges were adding up my score,
It looked to me I needed two points more.
They walked away and were still writing,
And so my fingernails I started biting.
Then came the time of the ribbons,
There were only three to be given.
Next I heard the judges say,
Katrina has won first place today.
And who could believe that first place prize,
Was a huge jar of one hundred one dragonflies!

Katrina Scheidecker

St. Charles School
Syracuse, NY
Nominated by fifth grade teacher Sue Migon

Losing A Very Close Friend

When you lose a close friend,
You never think you will be fine again.
Tossing and turning thinking of them.
Wondering... will I ever see them again?
Sitting peacefully, thinking of them.
It is hard -- we all know that.
Worrying, scared,
Not knowing what's going to happen.
Do they you wonder?
Do they even care?
Do they, you wonder.
But... I figured out I'll still wonder.
I will always know that I still care!!

Nicole Frajda

St. Charles School
Syracuse, NY
Nominated by fifth grade teacher Cheryl Wilday

Toys 'R' Us

One day I went to Toys 'R' Us,
On a big old yellow bus.
When the bus had arrived, I was asleep,
In a good dream, so very deep.
I finally awoke with a start
To see that the bus was about to part.
I stood up and ran for the door,
But I tripped on my shoelace and fell on the floor.
I screamed to the driver, "Get me off the bus!
I want to get to Toys 'R' Us!"
He said, "OK,
Whatever you say."
I finally got off the bus,
And looked at good ol' Toys 'R' Us.
The only problem was on the door,
There was a sign, close to the floor.
It said, "Closed at 9 p.m."
"Just my luck," I said. "It is 9:01 p.m."

Nicholas J. Butler

St. Charles School
Syracuse, NY
Nominated by fifth grade teacher Dru Pellizzari

Winter Fun

In winter when it's cold outside,
I take my sled for a ride.
Even when it's ten below,
Down the hill I will go.

Or maybe I will go and skate,
On a frozen pond or lake.
Ice-skating is very fun,
I'll skate for two hours before I'm done.

Or maybe I will get my skis,
And race down the hill trying not to freeze.
As I race down the slope,
I think about the Olympics with hope.

So in the winter months ahead,
Instead of complaining about the cold you dread,
Come with me and have some fun,
And the time of your life will have begun.

Jenna Marcellus

John E. Joy Elementary School
Rome, NY
Nominated by fifth grade teacher Lucille Merical

Summer

I love to play outside in the summer,
When I can't go out it's a great big bummer.
I like the summer better than winter or fall,
Because in the summer I can play baseball.
Mosquitoes and bugs, now those I don't like,
But I like it a lot when I can ride my bike.
Summer is nice but sometimes it's hot,
Now that's another thing I don't quite like a lot.
An amusement park is where I like to go,
There are rides and booths and sometimes a show.
In the summertime when you go out to play,
Remember this and hear me say:
Summer is my very favorite season,
And I don't have to have a reason.

Christine Aubry

John E. Joy Elementary School
Rome, NY
Nominated by fifth grade teacher Lucille Merical

My Brother

My brother thinks he's the bomb.
He says he's always calm.
His name is Dan.
But I don't think he's the man.
I don't think he has any fans.
He's kinda cool.
He even stays in school.
He's no fool.
At least that's what he said in the pool.

Alyssa Lamascolo

John E. Joy Elementary School
Rome, NY
Nominated by fifth grade teacher Lucille Merical

The Hummingbird

I once saw a hummingbird that buzzed like a bee,
It flew around and around, all wild and free.
The bird dove down to a very colorful flower,
It wanted some nectar so much
that it used all its power.

The hummingbird flew near the white-yellow daisy,
There was no nectar so he started to act crazy.
A bee zoomed down to the hummingbird's side,
And asked if he could hop on for a ride.

They flew around for about the whole day,
And both decided they weren't going to stay.
Suddenly they found a honeysuckle flower,
And ate all the nectar
realizing it was very sweet not sour!

Kevin David

Faith Fellowship Christian School
Watertown, NY
Nominated by fifth grade teacher Laura Cavallario

Fresh Air

When I go outside to see lots of things,
I see mountains, fountains, and big fat bees,
I hear chirp, bizz, buzz, and ouch oooo eehhh,
Then I get scared and I run away speedily.

Justin Reeves

Faith Fellowship Christian School
Watertown, NY
Nominated by fifth grade teacher Laura Cavallario

The Pandas

Pandas are dying every day,
But there is one that survived in a special way.
She was unknown for a while,
But when they realized she was alive
It made them smile!
Bai Yun was her name,
She loved to play games.
She had a baby
Unknown? Maybe.
Hua Mei was what they named the little cub,
When she was born she was pink, hairy,
And a little tub.
Now they both sit together in a zoo.
I am glad and bet Bai Yun is too!

For: Megan Murphy
Happy Birthday!

Tedra McDougal

South Jefferson Central School
Adams Center, NY
Nominated by fifth grade teacher Mrs. Piddock

Nature

Trees are green.
Grass is too.
Birds fly high in the sky that is light blue.
Flowers blue, purple, pink, yellow, white, and red.
All bundled up just like a bed.
Colors of the rainbow.
Clouds that bow down to you and me.
The wind whistles a lullaby.
As we say good night.

Casey McMahon

West End School
Lynbrook, NY
Nominated by fifth grade teacher Albert Marrazzo

Autumn In The Garden

The leaves fall to the ground
With graceful dips to the freezing earth below.
The wind blows slowly
Rustling the dying leaves
Urging them to break away from holding twigs.
The leaves are colors of red, orange, and yellow.
A rainbow could never compete with these leaves.
And the sky is growing dark
With colors of red and violet
And the sun slowly slips away.

Elizabeth Grace

New Windsor School
New Windsor, NY
Nominated by fifth grade teacher Linda Mangan

Leaves, Leaves...

Leaves, leaves, I'm a leaf of a sassafras tree.
And in the fall, when the wind blows
I hope I don't go down to the ground,
and just hang around 'til winter comes near
and then I fear I will then fade away.

Jessica Lallier

St. James School
Gouverneur, NY
Nominated by fifth grade teacher Susan Lillie

Snakes, Snakes, Snakes

Ugly snakes
Short snakes
Creepy, slithering, slimy snakes
Harmless, garden, rock snakes
Those are just a few.

Black snakes
White snakes
Orange, striped spotted snakes
Poison, biting, climbing snakes
Fast snakes, too!

Slow snakes
Fat snakes
And don't forget hungry snakes
Last of all
Best of all
I like long snakes!

Nichole Lindsley

Unadilla Elementary School
Otego, NY
Nominated by fifth grade teacher Maureen Gregory